The Story of America

IMMIGRATION AND MIGRATION

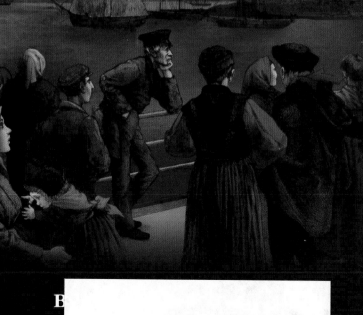

Please visit our Web site, www.garethstevens.com. For a free color catalog of all our high-quality books, call toll free 1-800-542-2595 or fax 1-877-542-2596.

Library of Congress Cataloging-in-Publication Data

Roza, Greg.
 Immigration and migration / Greg Roza.
   p. cm. — (The story of America)
 Includes index.
 ISBN 978-1-4339-4769-8 (pbk.)
 ISBN 978-1-4339-4770-7 (6-pack)
 ISBN 978-1-4339-4768-1 (library binding)
 1. United States—Emigration and immigration—History—Juvenile literature. I. Title.
 JV6450.R69 2011
 304.8'73—dc22

                              2010038390

First Edition

Published in 2011 by
Gareth Stevens Publishing
111 East 14th Street, Suite 349
New York, NY 10003

Copyright © 2011 Gareth Stevens Publishing

Designer: Daniel Hosek
Editor: Therese Shea

Photo credits: Cover, p. 1 FPG/Getty Images; p. 4 Rischgitz/Hulton Archive/Getty Images; p. 6 Kean Collection/Getty Images; pp. 7, 8–9, 16, 18, 19, 22–23, 24 MPI/Getty Images; p. 9 (Penn) Buyenlarge/Getty Images; pp. 10, 12–13, 17 Stock Montage/Getty Images; p. 14 Library of Congress, Prints and Photographs Division; p. 20 Archive Holdings Inc./Getty Images; p. 21 Shutterstock.com; p. 26 Moore Dunn/Hulton Archive/Getty Images; p. 29 Alex Wong/Getty Images.

Printed in the United States of America

CPSIA compliance information: Batch #CW11GS: For further information contact Gareth Stevens, New York, New York at 1-800-542-2595.

Contents

Words in the glossary appear in **bold** type the first time they are used in the text.

On the Move

Migration is movement from one place to another. Immigration is the migration of people into a new country. An immigrant moves into a country from another one to settle in the new land. The label is often used to describe people who have left their native country to settle in a new country. Once they are settled, they may migrate in search of work or a better life.

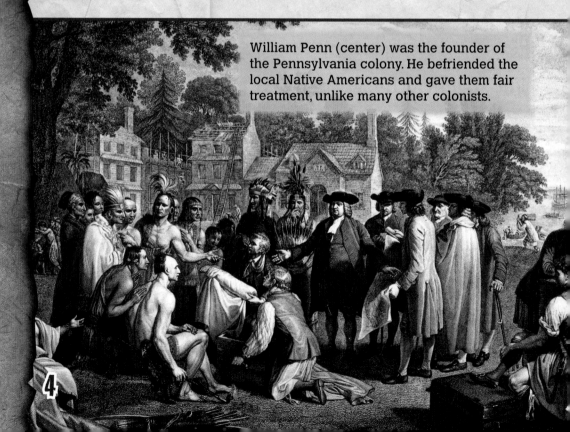

William Penn (center) was the founder of the Pennsylvania colony. He befriended the local Native Americans and gave them fair treatment, unlike many other colonists.

From the first days of European settlements in North America, immigration and migration have helped shape the country today called the United States. Thanks to these travelers, the United States transformed from a young country into a modern world power in just 400 years. Today, however, immigration is a hot issue of **debate** in the United States.

Native American Migration

Long before Europeans "discovered the New World," many Native American groups with different cultures and languages lived across North America. About 20,000 years ago, perhaps earlier, the first people migrated from Asia to North America. They crossed a narrow stretch of land that existed at the time called the Bering Land Bridge. Some settled in northern areas, while others continued south. By the time European explorers arrived in the Americas in the late 1400s, as many as 18 million Native Americans lived in North America.

Bering Land Bridge

North America

Asia

Early Migrations

After the initial European exploration of the "New World," Europeans began settling along the eastern coast. They came for several reasons. The first settlements in North America were little more than military bases. In 1565, Spain founded St. Augustine in today's state of Florida. It became the first permanent, continually inhabited European colony in North America.

By the late 1800s, St. Augustine had become a popular resort for wealthy vacationers.

Soon after St. Augustine, other settlements took root along the northeastern coast. Established in 1607, the Jamestown settlement became the foundation for the Virginia colony. Most of the settlers seeking fortune found hardship instead. In 1620, a group of Pilgrims—including Puritans seeking religious freedom—arrived near Plymouth, Massachusetts. These settlements were just the first of many that flourished despite the initial difficulties presented by life in North America.

The Slave Trade

The slave trade brought many Africans to the colonies of North America beginning in 1619. These were immigrants of another kind. They were forced to leave their homeland and freedom to travel to the colonies. Once there, they were made to do backbreaking labor for no money. Most were beaten and whipped, and many died. Families were broken apart. Many modern African Americans are **descendants** of African slaves.

DID YOU KNOW?

Ownership of St. Augustine changed hands over the years. At times, it was a settlement with few people. Other times, it was a lively port with thousands of immigrants.

European immigrants continued to come to the colonies of North America hoping for a better life. They came from all over Europe. Many made the difficult journey for the promise of cheap farmland. A great number were **indentured servants**. In exchange for passage to the colonies, they agreed to work for a certain number of years for the person who paid for their journey. At the end of that time, they were granted small plots of land for their own use. The indentured-servant system often determined where immigrant families settled.

This picture shows slaves and indentured servants working on a tobacco plantation in the 1700s.

Wealthy immigrants established large farms called plantations. Much land in the southern British colonies was used for cotton and tobacco plantations. Wealthy landowners came knowing they could make use of the cheap labor provided by indentured servants and slaves.

William Penn and Pennsylvania

After receiving a large piece of North American land from King Charles II, William Penn came to the colonies with the idea of creating a **utopia**. Penn was a Quaker who believed his "holy experiment" would become the "seed of a nation." He was right. Many of Penn's ideas for governing his colony influenced the writing of the U.S. Constitution. The population of the colony grew quickly. When Penn died in 1718, more than 40,000 people lived there.

William Penn

DID YOU KNOW?

In 1984, William Penn was declared an honorary citizen of the United States.

The Growing Nation

In 1783, England and the newly formed United States signed the Treaty of Paris, officially ending the American Revolution. The treaty made the Mississippi River the western U.S. border. The government quickly passed laws to encourage citizens to settle in western lands. Many settlers were given land that had belonged to Native Americans. The frontier continuously edged westward.

Many historians consider the Louisiana Purchase to be President Jefferson's greatest achievement while in office.

DID YOU KNOW?

Some of the first U.S. citizens to migrate to the Mississippi River were businessmen. They bought boats to transport people and goods on the river.

The Land Ordinance of 1785

After the American Revolution, the federal government quickly passed land ordinances, or laws, to help plan future states. The Land Ordinance of 1785 established a method of dividing up the formerly British land north and west of the Ohio River into areas called townships. Eventually, this territory became the states of Ohio, Indiana, Illinois, Michigan, and Wisconsin. Many Americans were eager to buy land there. However, the federal government faced several problems, including **squatters** and Native Americans who refused to leave.

In 1803, the United States purchased the Louisiana Territory from France. This doubled the size of the country. President Thomas Jefferson was eager to gain control of the Mississippi River and the port city of New Orleans. It wasn't long before river settlements—such as St. Louis in Missouri and Memphis in Tennessee—flourished as U.S. citizens migrated west.

Louisiana Territory

Mass Migration

The first era of mass migration into the United States began in the 1820s. The American economy had begun to grow strong. The promise of plentiful, cheap farmland was a big draw for poor European farmers.

Wars between European countries had ended by 1815. Soldiers returning home discovered things were changing. The **Industrial Revolution** made traditional agricultural practices less important in many areas. As

European Mormons—shown here at an immigration station in New York—were just one of many groups seeking religious freedom in the United States.

a result, many soldiers returning from the war felt as if they needed to move elsewhere, and the United States was a promising idea.

Many immigrants to the United States chose to stay in eastern cities. They often grouped together in neighborhoods, some of which survive to this day. Others migrated to the Midwest to find cheap farmland.

The Irish Potato Famine

In 1845, disease began killing Ireland's potatoes, one of the nation's main food sources. Over 6 years, more than 1 million people starved to death in what was called the Irish Potato Famine. Another 1 million left for the United States. Most lived in very poor conditions in eastern cities where it was hard to find jobs. They were often treated poorly. In time, however, Irish immigrants and their descendants became an important force in the industrial growth of the United States.

DID YOU KNOW?

From the 1820s to the 1880s, about 15 million immigrants came to the United States. These immigrants contributed to a growing workforce

Manifest Destiny

By the 1840s, the idea of "Manifest Destiny" had become a popular American ideal. Many Americans believed that it was the United States' destiny to stretch across North America from the Atlantic Ocean to the Pacific. More land meant more resources and more money.

U.S. forces were largely successful against Mexico during the U.S.-Mexican War. Here, General Zachary Taylor's army defeats Mexican troops at the Battle of Buena Vista.

The U.S. government used the belief in Manifest Destiny to justify political and military actions. In 1845, the United States **annexed** the Republic of Texas, which wanted to become a U.S. state. This heightened hostilities between the United States and Mexico, which also wanted Texas. After winning the U.S.-Mexican War in 1848, the United States claimed the Mexican land in the Southwest, as far west as California. Manifest Destiny had become a reality. The result was thousands of square miles of land open for U.S. migration.

DID YOU KNOW?

With the Gadsden Purchase from Mexico in 1853, the current U.S.-Mexican border was established. Mainland United States had taken on its present shape.

Trail of Tears

Even before Manifest Destiny had taken root, some U.S. lawmakers believed the United States was destined to grow larger. Native Americans were often the victims of U.S. policies. By 1837, 46,000 Native Americans had been forced to migrate west of the Mississippi River from their homelands in the Southeast. About 4,000 Cherokee Indians died during the removal. Their route and journey became known as the Trail of Tears.

Paths West

Completed in 1825, the Erie Canal allowed people to travel more quickly and cheaply than ever before. It connected the once-distant locations of New York City and Buffalo, New York. Buffalo and other small settlements along the canal grew quickly as people

On May 10, 1869, the final spike of the transcontinental railroad was driven at Promontory Point, Utah.

migrated west. Many of these were immigrants who had only recently arrived in New York City.

Between 1841 and 1869, pioneers used the Oregon Trail and other trails to travel to the Pacific Northwest in search of fortune and adventure. By the 1840s, about 600 miles (965 km) of railroad track stretched from eastern cities to growing towns along the Mississippi River. The first transcontinental railroad was completed in 1869. Finally, transportation linked the eastern and western United States. The stream of migration to the West became a river.

The California Gold Rush

After gold was discovered in California in 1848, people from around the globe rushed to the area in search of riches. Some people from the eastern United States traveled by land. Others traveled by ship around South America. Both routes were dangerous and took many months. Miners from Mexico and South America migrated to California. Many Chinese miners arrived by boat from Asia. Between 1848 and 1852, California's population swelled from about 15,000 to nearly 225,000 people.

DID YOU KNOW?

Between 1820 and 1850, nearly 4 million Americans migrated to the western United States.

The American Civil War

In 1865, the North won the American Civil War. Many of the South's farms, cities, and railroads had been destroyed. Slavery was outlawed, and Southern plantation owners were forced to find new ways to conduct business. There was a drop

In this painting, Abraham Lincoln reads the Emancipation Proclamation, which stated that all Southern slaves were to be set free.

in the importance of Southern agriculture and a rise in Northern industrial jobs. Many workers migrated to Northern cities to find work. Many ex-slaves also fled to the Northern states, although some stayed behind to work on farms that continued to function.

While many Southerners migrated north, thousands of Southern farmers went to Brazil. Brazilian officials at the time were searching for immigrants with knowledge about farming, especially cotton. These American **emigrants** were able to establish profitable plantations in a different country.

◄ Harriet Tubman ►

The Underground Railroad

Prior to the American Civil War, members of the abolition movement helped slaves escape to the North and Canada. Abolitionists set up secret "way stations" along routes to the North. This system of hideaways became known as the Underground Railroad. Former slave Harriet Tubman was the most famous "conductor" on the Underground Railroad. Between 1810 and 1850, approximately 100,000 slaves used these secret routes to migrate north.

DID YOU KNOW?

Between 1850 and 1859, Harriet Tubman led over 300 slaves to freedom.

A Flood of Immigrants

The number of immigrants entering the United States increased dramatically in the 1880s. The introduction of steam-powered ships made the trip across the Atlantic faster and less expensive. More immigrants came from southern and eastern Europe than ever before. The number of immigrants from Asia and the Middle East increased as well. In the 1880s,

Hundreds of immigrants hail the Statue of Liberty upon entering New York Harbor.

9 percent of the population of Norway came to the United States! Many of these people settled in urban centers across the country, where they contributed greatly to the growth of industry and **commerce**.

In the late 1800s and early 1900s, numerous anti-Jewish riots—called pogroms—swept across Russia and Poland. Tens of thousands of Jews fled the violence and came to America. The majority settled in New York City.

Ellis Island

Ellis Island in New York Harbor was once the busiest immigration station in the country. The island is named for Samuel Ellis, the man who owned it in the 1770s. New York State sold the island to the federal government in 1808. The government built Fort Gibson there and used it as an immigration station from 1892 to 1954. Today, it's home to an immigration museum and is part of the Statue of Liberty National Monument.

DID YOU KNOW?

Between 1892 and 1954, more than 12 million immigrants passed through Ellis Island.

◀ **Statue of Liberty**

Immigrants from Europe and other locations who were fleeing poverty hoped to find the United States "paved with streets of gold." The reality they discovered, however, was far different from the rumors they had heard. The great majority of immigrants ended up living in crowded urban areas where there weren't enough jobs for everyone. Many remained in poverty.

However, the flood of immigration that began in the late 1800s and lasted into the early 1900s helped the country grow into a world power.

Two brothers actually rode bikes during the Oklahoma Land Rush! However, they weren't there for land. They were just there to watch.

Immigrants helped to build railroads, power lines, gas lines, roads, bridges, and tunnels all across the country. Thanks in part to millions of immigrant laborers, the United States became a leading producer of steel, coal, oil, automobiles, electrical equipment, and many other modern necessities.

The Great Oklahoma Land Rush

In 1828, the U.S. government set aside land called "Indian Territory" for Native Americans. Today, this area is known as Oklahoma. Starting in the 1880s, the U.S. government opened up sections of Indian Territory for white settlement. The largest "land rush" came in 1893. On September 16, 1893, a cannon fired at noon, and 100,000 settlers raced to claim 42,000 plots of land. Although not every settler claimed land that day, many chose to settle nearby.

DID YOU KNOW?

Many of Oklahoma's settlers earned the name "Sooners" for entering the state before receiving the government's permission

Fears and Legislation

Prior to the 1880s, the majority of immigrants that came to the United States hailed from northern and western Europe. However, throughout the 1880s, the number of immigrants from eastern and southern Europe, the Middle East, and Asia increased rapidly.

Chinese immigrants are attacked by white coal miners in Rock Springs, Wyoming.

These people had customs and languages that were unfamiliar to Americans. Many U.S. citizens—particularly wealthy white people—felt immigration was beginning to pose a threat to the security of the country.

In 1882, Congress passed the Chinese Exclusion Act as a response to pressure from California to stop the rapidly increasing numbers of Chinese immigrants. The law prevented Chinese laborers from entering the country for 10 years. It represented an extreme change in the U.S. government's position on immigration.

The Immigration Restriction League

In the late 1880s, many employers were hiring immigrant laborers from eastern and southern Europe because they worked for less pay than American workers. In 1894, several graduates of Harvard University in Massachusetts believed this growing immigrant population was harming the American way of life. They formed the Immigration Restriction League, hoping to stem the tide of immigrants they considered inferior to themselves. They urged Congress to use tests to limit the number of immigrants who could become citizens.

DID YOU KNOW?

In 1892, the Chinese Exclusion Act was renewed for another 10 years.

In the early 1900s, new laws stopped immigrants with diseases and criminal records from entering the country. Limits were soon applied to other groups of immigrants, such as those who were thought to be **anarchists**. After the outbreak of World War I in 1914, U.S. citizens became even more uneasy about allowing immigrants into the country. Increased **nationalism** and fear of foreigners led to more legislation limiting immigration.

Immigrants at Ellis Island had to go through numerous medical tests to get into the country.

In 1924, Congress passed the Johnson-Reed Act, which set a yearly limit of 150,000 on immigrants from outside the Western Hemisphere. That total was divided into quotas, or a proportion of immigrants from each country. The larger the population already in the United States, the larger the quota. This was an advantage for western Europeans, who already had a large presence in the United States.

DID YOU KNOW?

In 1924, British, German, and Irish immigrants made up more than half of the 150,000 limit set by the Johnson-Reed Act. In comparison, 100 or fewer immigrants from Turkey were allowed into the United States.

Quotas of the Johnson-Reed Act

The Johnson-Reed Act of 1924 was mainly designed to stop immigration from eastern and southern Europe. This table shows many of the annual immigration quotas defined by the act.

country	quota
Germany	51,227
Great Britain	34,007
Ireland	28,567
Sweden	9,561
Norway	6,453
Poland	5,982
France	3,954
Italy	3,845
Denmark	2,789
Russia	2,248
Romania	603
Spain	131
Greece	100
Turkey	100

The Twentieth Century and Beyond

As the children of immigrants who had arrived in the United States between 1880 and 1914 became voters, fears about immigration began to change. While many Americans still feared foreigners throughout the **Cold War**, scholars and scientists from Europe continued to come to the United States throughout the mid-1900s. The United States also became a popular destination for **refugees** in search of a better life, regardless of immigration laws.

In 1965, the Hart-Celler Act changed immigration law in the United States and kicked off a new flood of immigration. This new act did

Timeline

1565	1783	1825	1837	1845
Spain founds St. Augustine settlement	Treaty of Paris recognizes the United States as an independent country	Erie Canal completed	Forced migration of Cherokees on Trail of Tears	Irish Potato Famine causes mass U.S. immigration

away with the quota system and put all immigrants on equal footing. It was designed to end **discrimination** in immigration law, just as the civil rights movement of the 1950s and 1960s sought to end discrimination within U.S. society.

Today, illegal immigration is a hot issue. Should illegal immigrants be allowed jobs and the rights of U.S. citizens?

1848	**1869**	**1892**	**1894**	**1965**
Gold is discovered in California	First transcontinental railroad is completed	Ellis Island begins use as an immigration station	Immigration Restriction League is formed	Hart-Celler Act abolishes immigration quota system

Glossary

anarchist: someone who rejects the need for a system of government in society

annex: to take over an area and make it part of a larger territory

Cold War: the nonviolent conflict between the United States and the Union of Soviet Socialist Republics (USSR) during the second half of the 20th century

commerce: the large-scale buying and selling of goods and services

debate: a prolonged argument or public discussion

descendant: someone related to a person who lived in the past

discrimination: unfair treatment of a group, usually because of race, ethnicity, age, religion, or gender

emigrant: someone who leaves his or her native country to live in another country

indentured servant: one who signs a contract agreeing to work for a set period of time in exchange for money and other benefits

Industrial Revolution: an era of social and economic change marked by advances in technology and science

nationalism: loyalty and devotion to one's nation and promotion of its culture as superior to others

refugee: someone who is seeking a safe place to live, especially during a time of war

squatter: someone who settles on land without consent

utopia: a perfect place or state

For More Information

BOOKS

Bailey, Rayna. *Immigration and Migration*. New York, NY: Facts On File, 2008.

Peacock, Louise. *At Ellis Island: A History in Many Voices*. New York, NY: Atheneum Books for Young Readers, 2007.

Sioux, Tracee. *Immigrants in Colonial America*. New York, NY: PowerKids Press, 2004.

WEB SITES

Destination America: U.S. Immigration
www.pbs.org/destinationamerica/usim.html
Visit this PBS site for facts, stories, and resources about U.S. immigration.

Ellis Island
www.ellisisland.org
The Ellis Island Web site has information about the island's history, immigration, and much more.

Index